ANY OLD CLOTHES
YOU DON'T NEED ANY MORE?
WE'LL SELL THEM HERE,
AT THE SECOND-HAND STORE.

DONATIONS

DONATIONS
NEEDED

Donate

stuff
to
donate

For Mum and Dad,
who've always encouraged me to dream
and for Billy, who stitched this story together.

R.T.

To Roux & Autumn, who fill every
day with endless sparkle.

P.C.

OXFORD
UNIVERSITY PRESS

Great Clarendon Street, Oxford OX2 6DP

Oxford University Press is a department of the University of Oxford.
It furthers the University's objective of excellence in research, scholarship,
and education by publishing worldwide. Oxford is a registered trade mark
of Oxford University Press in the UK and in certain other countries

Text © Robert Tregoning 2023
Illustration © Pippa Curnick 2023

The moral rights of the author and artist have been asserted

Database right Oxford University Press (maker)

First published 2023

British Library Cataloguing in Publication Data available

ISBN: 978-0-19-278358-5

1 3 5 7 9 10 8 6 4 2

Printed in China

Paper used in the production of this book is a natural,
recyclable product made from wood grown in sustainable forests.
The manufacturing process conforms to the environmental
regulations of the country of origin

Robert Tregoning

Pippa Curnick

THE DRESS IN THE WINDOW

SHACK

SECOND-HAND

MUSIC LESSONS
Call Mr. Jeeves

Closed

OXFORD
UNIVERSITY PRESS

One afternoon, on the high street in town,
a boy, with his mum, saw a **sparkling** gown.

SECOND-HAND THR

It hung in the window of Second-hand Thread,
all glowing, all flowing, all dazzling and red.

It seemed to call out as the boy tried to pass.
He stopped. And he pressed his small nose to the glass.
He gazed at the garment, with eyes open wide,
and noticed his heart disco dancing inside.

£25

There, in that moment, the boy made a wish:
to put on that dress and to swirl and to swish.
He took in the sequins, from shoulder to floor,
and wondered, what life did this dress live before?

Was it once worn
by a **star** of the screen,
who walked the red carpet
and **stole** every scene?

TOP
SECRET

Or maybe the **greatest** of all the world's spies once used it as part of a **perfect** disguise?

Was it once worn
in a room filled with jazz,
by a spotlit performer,
who sang with pizazz?

Or was it once shown
by a fashion designer
whose runways had never
seen anything finer?

Now, in this window, it stood on display,
for anyone passing and willing to pay.
'Maybe,' said Mum, 'if you do a few chores
and save up some pennies, that dress could be yours.'

Nothing would stop him!
Whatever it took!

He'd wash, clean and tidy,
he'd carry and cook.

He'd ask all the neighbours
who lived on their road   if dogs could be walked
                                  or if lawns could be mowed.

At house number seven he helped Mrs Mack,
who found housework tricky because of her back.

At house number twenty he washed an old car
and polished it up so it shone like a star.

At house number thirty he swept up the leaves
and watered the flowers to help Mr Jeeves.

At house number forty he brushed the dogs' tails.
He washed them and dried them and clipped all their nails.

He counted his coins and he'd reached twenty-four
when kindly, the tooth fairy left him one more.

So now with enough, the boy lay in his bed
and danced in his dreams wearing sequins of red.

Next morning came with a hug and some toast.
'Happy Birthday,' said Mum,
'to the boy I love most!'

Happy Birthday

JAM

She took him to school, saying, 'See you at three.
We'll walk home through town back for presents and tea.'

SCHOOL

Three o'clock came, not a moment too soon:
the boy had been counting the seconds since noon.
He knew that they'd walk past the dress of his dreams.
He leapt in excitement and burst at the seams!

Over the playground and through the school gate.
He thought of the dress and he just couldn't wait.

'Hang on!' Mum cried, as she tried to keep pace.
Her son was now running as if in a race.

MUSIC SHACK SECOND-HAND

The dress in the window was just round the bend
and this time, the boy had his savings to spend.

Feeling a thrill that he couldn't quite bear.
He looked through the window . . .

The dress was not there!

SALE

20% OFF SUITS

The boy's heart stopped dancing.
It sank to the floor.

Never.
Had he.
Wanted.
Anything.
More.

Mum held his hand as she said, 'Never mind.
Your presents are waiting—who knows what you'll find?'

When they got home all the neighbours were there
with gifts for the boy and a big cake to share.
The boy thanked them all as he offered them tea,
then Mum smiled and said, 'Here's your present from me.'

She passed him the parcel. It wasn't a book.
It felt soft and squishy. The boy's fingers shook.
He thought of the dress—but he knew it had gone—
he peeled back the paper and something bright shone.

A **shimmer** of sequins, a **glimmer** of red.
'I bought it before someone else did,' Mum said.
'I couldn't risk waiting, they only had one.
One **beautiful** dress   for my **beautiful** son.'

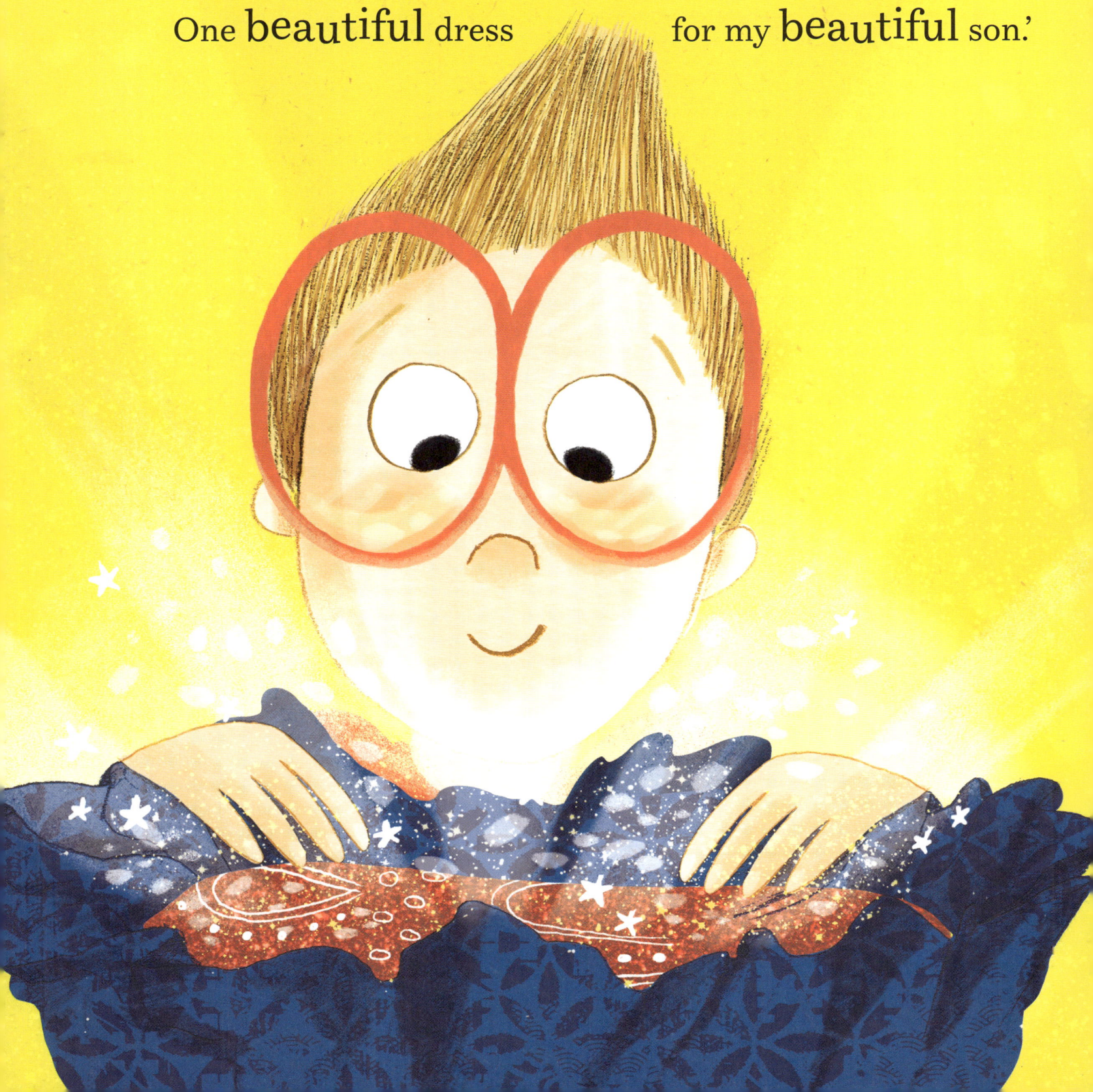

The boy tried it on and he smiled as he spun.
He loved how it sparkled—like light from the sun.
He danced through the house and he filled it with joy.
And everyone wanted to dance with the boy.

He danced round the garden and out in the road,
he swirled and he twirled as his happiness flowed.
He smiled at his mum and she smiled back at him . . .

Her son, in his dress,
filled with love to the brim.